The Ready Book

The Ready Book

Quickly find important family information
in the event of emergency or death

Catherine I. Katz

THAT'S A PLENTY FARM PRESS   NORTHAMPTON

Catherine Katz likes to be organized. Now retired, she spent her work life managing relationships for schools and school-software developers. Her focus took a turn in 2007, when, in response to climate change predictions, Catherine and her husband of 50 years, Michael, began preparing for an uncertain future. They bought a three-acre floodplain cornfield that had been farmed for 1000 years and set out to learn about permaculture farming and how to grow their own food. In 2011, their farm, That's A Plenty Farm, evolved into the first pollinator habitat in western Massachusetts to be funded in part by the USDA's Natural Resources Conservation Service. In 2012, they downsized their carbon footprint by moving into a tiny house on the farm; tiny house living has proven to be comfortable and satisfying. The farm's focus is sustainability—ready for whatever happens—with a goal to eventually have a net positive effect on family, community, and the creatures with whom we share the planet. Learn more about the farm at thatsaplentyfarm.com.

That's A Plenty Farm Press, Northampton 01060
© 2019 by That's A Plenty Farm Press
All Rights Reserved
First edition published 2019
Prinnted in the United States of America

ISBN: 978-1-7338020-0-0

This book is dedicated to my mother,
Anamary Evans Compere Bowden,
who helped us help her.

"There was something else my mother did that I've always remembered: 'Always look for the helpers,' she'd tell me. 'There's always someone who is trying to help.' I did, and I came to see that the world is full of doctors and nurses, police and firemen, volunteers, neighbors and friends who are ready to jump in to help when things go wrong."

— Fred Rogers
As quoted in the *St. Louis Dispatch,* 2004

Table of Contents

Preface ix
Acknowledgements xi
How a READY BOOK Can Help Your Family xiii

The Three Most Important Documents
Health Care Proxy 1
Durable Power of Attorney 5
Will & Memorandum 7

PEOPLE
Gather These Documents 13
Record This Information 15
List Extended Family Contacts 19

PLACES
Gather Documents & Keys 21
Record This Information 23
Include Place History 25

THINGS
Take a Photo Inventory 27
Gather These Documents 29
Plan for Precious Belongings 31

MONEY
Make a Basic Financial Plan 33
Have Cash on Hand 35
Gather These Documents 37
Document Your Assets 39
Document Your Liabilities 45

Help Family Access Your Devices & Data 51

In Case of Death: CHECKLISTS
To Do IMMEDIATELY 53
To Do TWO WEEKS Later 57
To Do 6 WEEKS – 6 MONTHS After 61

Where Should You Store Your READY BOOK? 63

Preface

This guide was written out of gratitude to my mother for teaching us an important lesson: One of the best gifts you can give your loved ones is to organize your legal documents and key personal information in a way that will be useful to them when an emergency strikes.

My mother had planned years in advance for the sudden medical emergency that would eventually end her life. Of course, she could not know the exact manner or moment of her death, but she had organized herself years earlier in anticipation of the inevitable—in order to not be a burden to her children.

And then it happened. Following a Christmas dinner with the family, my mother, age 90, didn't feel well. She agreed to be taken to the hospital, not realizing she would never return home again. Over the next 42 days before she died there, my sisters and I kept her company around the clock, while my mother made a series of major decisions with her physicians about her own treatment. Even so, her death seemed sudden, and we "girls" had tasks to perform.

"Look in the little green suitcase in my closet," she had said. "Everything you need is there."

Later, after I had returned to my own home hundreds of miles away, I thought of how grateful I was to my Mom the moment I opened her little green suitcase and found her titles and will, her wishes and proxies and passwords. I became determined to do the same for my own family. I collected our core documents and then showed all of my next-of-kin where to find them. And I am relieved to see that now our adult children are collecting their own sets of files.

We're all making it easier for our loved ones to cope in an emergency. You will be glad to have taken the time to think about ways you can help your family manage difficult events in the future. The ideas in this book are not complex, but designed for moments when people may feel overwhelmed and not able to take a step in any direction.

If you found The READY BOOK helpful, please consider leaving a review on the site where you purchased it. Reviews from readers go a long way in bringing a book to the attention of others who may also be helped. I also welcome any of your own ideas as to how to improve this process and make The READY BOOK even more useful. You can reach me through the website of our family farm, where we work toward pollinator health and soil sustainability: thatsaplentyfarm.com.

Catherine I. Katz, March 2019

Acknowledgements

I am grateful for the ideas contributed to this book by: my husband, Michael, who was a great friend to Anamary; our children, Jenny and Josh; grandsons Isaac and Emerson; son-in-law and first responder Luc; Mom's sister, Susie; my sisters, Linda, Annie, and Mary; and our friends PK, Phoebe, and Ellen.

Jenny Katz-Brandoli has shaped The READY BOOK project as editor, designer, and technology director.

Thank you all.

INTRODUCTION
How a READY BOOK Can Help Your Family

What Are You Getting READY For?

By its very definition, an emergency means an event is unexpected and feels chaotic and stressful; it might prove to be a milestone in your family history. When you make reasonable preparation for an emergency, you can add a layer of calm and resilience for your family.

In an emergency, your loved ones will be making decisions. You can support them by collecting a small archive of personal documents and information, which will help your family make good decisions in bad circumstances. You can reduce the anxiety.

This READY BOOK will help you prepare for the following kinds of emergencies, by guiding you through the collection of relevant family data (permissions, access, identification) for the purpose of informed decision making:

Medical Emergency
Property Emergency
Financial Emergency
Death

Medical Emergency

A Medical Emergency may require life-and-death decision-making. Give your loved ones the power to take action.

WHAT IF your 21 year-old daughter needs emergency medical treatment but is not conscious or capable of giving consent? Who has the legal right to make decisions for her? What would she want?

About a month ago, my brother-in-law (who thought he was in excellent health) suffered a major heart attack. He was rushed to the Emergency Room, where a decision had to be made about treatment, and every minute was crucial. His son, who was with his dad in the ER, had a photo of the Health Care Proxy naming him an authorized decision-maker, on his phone, so the son was able to work with the medical team in forming a treatment strategy that reflected his father's wishes.

Property Emergency

A Property Emergency may require a sudden evacuation followed by a prolonged period of dislocation or rebuilding. Give your family easy access to supporting people and documents.

WHAT IF you've just been alerted you have 20 minutes to evacuate before fire destroys your home?

As I write this introduction, a dear friend is evacuating her home in California, as a wildfire has crested a ridge nearby. The fire was not near her town as they went to bed. At 3 a.m., alarms went off on their cellphones, the landline phone, and the television. They were awakened by blaring cries of "LEAVE NOW! LEAVE NOW!" They did not take any time to "think" as they left. Fortunately, they had put a folder of documents, their medications, and a change of clothes in the car before they went to bed, just in case. They were READY to GO.

Financial Emergency

A Financial Emergency may develop silently (electronically) and rapidly if the person who usually takes care of business is suddenly not able to do so. Provide your loved ones an overview of the family's finances so they can know what resources exist and avoid a crisis.

If I should die today, my Social Security check income will stop immediately—but the auto-payments of our mortgage and credit cards and health insurance will continue to be withdrawn from our bank accounts, electronically, without fanfare. My husband is not very involved in our day-to-day finances. If I am suddenly gone and he falls into depression (of course he would), it could be weeks before he thinks to look at the balance in our bank account. I intend to protect my spouse from falling into a Financial Emergency while he is mourning my loss.

Death

A Death in the family will require notifications, systematic cleaning of public records, and the dispersal of belongings according to the individual's wishes. These tasks can seem overwhelming; nevertheless some items need attention in the earliest days following the death.

"Turning off" all the connections of a formerly-alive person to the wide world can be daunting: Where to begin? What matters? Some tasks should be attended to within days of the death, especially to protect resources and prevent identity theft. The READY BOOK offers checklists so a family can easily work through tasks at the appropriate time without having to think of it themselves.

The Take-Away: You're Helping Your Family Manage an Emergency

If you're reading this book, it's likely that you're the person who usually takes care of business. You know where documents and accounts and passwords are, and you manage the details of the ebb and flow of your family's life. When an emergency suddenly strikes, maybe you'll be there to manage it. Or maybe, this time, YOU'll be the one in crisis and won't be in a position to manage things—which means that someone else will have to step in.

So, first things first: Start by collecting the most critical documents. The items that will have the biggest impact on your ability to deal with an emergency are your core legal permission forms: the HEALTH CARE PROXY and the DURABLE POWER OF ATTORNEY. Get these first. Now. Even if you do nothing else in this book, having these two forms for each adult will make you READY for an emergency.

Collect core documents and information in one central location and tell your loved ones where to find your collection. Give them access to the information they need to deal with your emergency; don't make them search.

Ask yourself: What information will my family need? The READY BOOK will help you collect a solid base of helpful documents and information.

Lower the stress level: Imagine your family's relief, finding all of your papers and information in one place. Make it portable—if necessary, you can grab it and GO.

Once you have your first two documents in place, filling the rest of your own READY BOOK is a straightforward process; this book will guide you, step-by-step, as you build your collection.

Chapter 1
Health Care Proxy

This is the MOST URGENT emergency document.

The Health Care Proxy is a simple legal document, specific to the state where you receive health care, in which you name a trusted person ("Agent"), and then a back-up person, to make health care decisions for you in the event you are not able to make decisions for yourself. This allows you to maintain control over your own care. This document is signed in the presence of witnesses, who also sign.

Get a signed and witnessed Health Care Proxy form for each individual in your immediate family who is 18 years or older.

Where To Get the Form

You can search online for a form legal in your state, or request a form from your physician.

What To Do with a Completed Form

Share a paper copy with each person designated as an agent for the individual.

Suggest that the agent also stores your proxy form in an accessible place on their phone, for instant access in an emergency—as a photo, for example.

Share a paper copy of the Health Care Proxy with the person's primary physician, who will add the form to the patient's medical file.

Keep a copy of each completed Health Care Proxy form in a brightly colored folder. This folder is the start of your READY BOOK.

You can keep forms for the other family members, or your adult children may choose to store their own documents.

Note: It is not good practice to send confidential files by email or text.

Why You Need a Health Care Proxy

When a person experiences a medical emergency and is suddenly not capable of making medical decisions for themselves, another person must make decisions for them. If we have not designated the person we want to speak for us, we relinquish control over life and death decisions to some unknown "other."

Whom do you most trust to decide on your behalf, in an emergency, whether you should live or die? Which person will do what YOU want, regardless of what choice they might make for themselves?

Individuals raised in the same family may have differing ideas about medical care, so do not assume that a child, sibling, or parent would make decisions the way you would. In order to ensure that your own wishes and preferences are honored, select an agent who will act on your own behalf, and then you make sure the agent understands your wishes. Remember, this agent will bear significant responsibility, such as if a physician determines that you are not able to make decisions for yourself, including perhaps making a decision to consent to or refuse any medical treatment, including treatment that could keep you alive by life support technology in a medical setting.

The freedom to make decisions for our own self is a right granted under law. Another person cannot just take away our right to make our own decisions, except in a court of law, so this legal document will ensure that your trusted person—the agent you name and no one else—is recognized as your decision-maker. Give this designated person their own copy of your Health Care Proxy, so they can prove they have authority if you are stricken. Ask them to take a photo of the document with their phone, so they have instant access to it. Keep your original Health Care Proxy in your READY BOOK binder. You can make photocopies of your completed Health Care Proxy form to give to medical facilities that request a copy for their files.

DO NOT relinquish your original Health Care Proxy document to anyone. Make copies.

In a Medical Emergency, if a person is conscious and able to communicate, the physician will discuss options and outcomes directly with the patient. My mother managed her own care right up to the very end—including her decision to end medical intervention. Nevertheless, my sisters and I used our status as Mom's Health Care Proxy to enter into conversations with Medicare and Mom's physicians. These conversations would have been prohibited by Hyppa privacy laws if we had not been her legally designated Health Care Proxies.

While a Health Care Proxy form is a legal document that names your primary and secondary agents, it does not specify treatment choices. It only says that you name this person to act on your behalf. You do not need to have any form that describes specific treatment; your proxy will make a decision if you cannot. Don't be shy about expressing your wishes to your agent; in fact, you are doing them a favor by making your wishes known to them ahead of time. Consider that this person will be VERY IMPORTANT to you when you are fully incapacitated and appreciate that they are assuming a huge responsibility.

"Shall we stop life support?"

Make sure your agent understands how you feel about extreme medical treatment. To assist you with this conversation (it's simpler than you may think), your physician can provide a simple form that asks you to consider a few different circumstances under which life support might be used.

Everyone 18 years of age or older should designate a Health Care Proxy.

Scan or photograph your Health Care Proxy form and share print and digital copies with your agent(s) immediately. If your agent is a smartphone user, ask them to add your documents to their phone in such a way that they will have access in case of emergency—for instance, as a saved picture in their photo library.

Again: It is not good practice to send confidential files by email or text.

Chapter 2
Durable Power of Attorney

This is the SECOND MOST URGENT emergency document.

The Durable Power of Attorney is a core legal document that ensures you have legally designated someone to make decisions on your behalf and take actions on your behalf if you are not able to do so. While the Health Care Proxy covers health care decisions, the Durable Power of Attorney covers all areas, including control of your finances such as making decisions about how much to spend for health care. These two documents may name the same agent, or, for example, if the Health Care Proxy agent is not skilled in money management, perhaps these agents will be two different people. Make sure your agents will be able to work well together according to your wishes on such decisions as "Should you enroll in a nursing home or enter into a contract for home health care?"

Anyone 21 years of age or older should have a Durable Power of Attorney prepared by an attorney.

The person you designate to be your attorney-in-fact should have an official copy of the completed Durable Power of Attorney form in their possession. Scan or photograph your Durable Power of Attorney and share both print and digital copies with your designated agent immediately. If your agent is a smartphone user, ask them to add your documents to their phone in a way they will have access in case of emergency.

Make your Attorney-in-fact aware of the READY BOOK.

Reminder: It is not good practice to send confidential files by email or text.

Where To Get the Form

Ask your attorney to draw up a Durable Power of Attorney for you. Discuss the powers granted by this document. Your attorney will ensure that the document reflects accurately your own situation. You can search online for a form legal in your state, but forms purchased online may not accurately match your particular situation.

What To Do with a Completed Form

Share a paper copy with the person designated as your "Agent" or "Attorney-in-fact."

Suggest that the attorney-in-fact also stores your Durable Power of Attorney form in an accessible place on their phone, for instant access in an emergency—as a photo, for example.

Your attorney will keep a copy of your Durable Power of Attorney.

Keep a copy of each Durable Power of Attorney in your brightly colored folder.

Make sure your loved ones know about this folder and where to find it. Keep the folder in a place where you can easily grab it in case of emergency.

You're better prepared already! This folder, with the Health Care Proxy and the Durable Power of Attorney inside, is READY to GO. These two forms are the start of your READY BOOK.

CHAPTER 3

Will & Memorandum

Each adult should have a simple Will and a hand-written Memorandum.

Who will care for your young children if you were to die? Who will be the next owners of the things and places and money you leave behind? You decide. You specify your wishes in your Last Will and Testament.

Don't burden your loved ones. WRITE A WILL. If you do not leave a Will and Memorandum, after your death "someone" will have to take the time to make an inventory of all your belongings and then go through a probate court proceeding to get them distributed fairly.

Spare them the trouble: Meet with an attorney to draw up a simple Will at the same time that you draw up a Health Care Proxy and a Durable Power of Attorney. These are all simple, straightforward legal documents.

Any parent of children under the age of 18 should specify in their Will the names and contact information for guardians of their minor children.

The purpose of a Will is for you to name beneficiaries of your estate. The legal process of probate transfers ownership from the deceased to their heirs. The process of probate can take months, or years. You can eliminate the need for probate by establishing joint ownership, naming beneficiaries, and leaving a clear Will and Memorandum.

Check your property titles for the term "Joint Tenancy with Rights of Survivorship." Any items that are owned jointly by you and some other person(s)—such as a real estate deed or a vehicle registration—do NOT go through probate, as their ownership is already established; the surviving joint owner already owns it.

A different option for bequeathing property is through a Living Trust. Ask your attorney if a Living Trust would be beneficial to you.

For all of your other belongings, you can make a hand-written, dated, and signed Memorandum to your Will that stipulates how your possessions should be distributed. Even a statement like, "My spouse and children shall inherit all of my belongings" is sufficient. Once you write a Memorandum, those items have clear owners and do not have to go through probate.

Items that are not jointly owned, that do not have named beneficiaries, or that are not specified in your Memorandum, will be distributed under the watchful eye of probate court. The process of probate is to ensure that a deceased person's things are distributed to new owners, fairly, according to the law, by the executor of the estate—who is a person legally confirmed by the Court.

You name an executor in your Will. (Note: The person named by you as executor may refuse the responsibility after your death by petitioning the court.) During probate, family members may step forward to make requests for items in the estate.

Be considerate of the family members who survive you: Downsize—now. Keeping too much stuff will burden your loved ones. Ask your family members if there are items they want to inherit, and then distribute the remainder gradually to organizations that will find new homes for your stuff—Goodwill or the Salvation Army, shelters, local charities, etc.

Destroy "private" items such as diaries. If you think a secret will cause your loved ones harm or unhappiness, then destroy such things. Make a bonfire, or shove it in a shredder.

Include online business websites, shopping carts, and payment processing platforms (such as PayPal, where income sits until the owner fetches it) in your Memorandum.

Should You Set Up a Living Trust?

Several advisors on the subject of estate planning suggest setting up a Living Trust. Consult with your attorney about whether a Living Trust is appropriate for you. Ask what happens if you sell an asset that is included in the Living Trust: What options do you have if you want to invest the proceeds of that sale in something new?

In our case—since we had established joint ownership for all our property—our attorney suggested we simply add a handwritten Memorandum to our Wills to cover all the rest of our things.

Make Sure All the Heirs You Intend to Inherit Will Actually Inherit

Check with your accountant and/or attorney to confirm that what you think will happen is what will actually happen with your assets when you die.

Our accountant gave this example:

• CURRENT STRATEGY: Parent and Adult Child 1 are joint owners of a bank account.

Parent intends that, upon her death, Child 1 will divide the balance of the account equally among all three children in the family. But, legally, when the parent dies, because Child 1 was joint owner with the parent and none of the other children was on the account, 100% of the balance becomes the property of Child 1. Child 1 can now do as she pleases, she owns all the money remaining in the deceased parent's account. Child 1 can distribute the money as the parent intended, or only some of the money ("I subtracted my expenses"), or none of the money to the other surviving children.

- BETTER STRATEGY: Parent opens a joint account with each Adult Child

To make sure each of her three children inherits as the parent intends, the parent could instead open three different bank accounts, and maintain in each account the amount the parent wants that child to inherit. Each child can be a co-owner/beneficiary on one of the parent's accounts.

Protect Your Assets Against Seizure by the Government to Offset Your Future Nursing Home Costs

Since we are talking about the fate of your life savings, ask your accountant and attorney for advice about your own particular circumstance, now, while you are alive and kicking. It is well worth it to meet with your accountant to learn what your options are, and what the tax implications are for your family.

Under most circumstances, the government will not seize your primary residence to cover (expensive!) long-term healthcare costs if the property is jointly owned by you and another person. So add a joint owner to your residential property deed, or set up a Living Trust through your attorney.

If you are now a widow/er, and have inherited assets from your spouse, you should work with your accountant to restructure your assets to meet your own long term goals and proactively anticipate the tax impact on your heirs.

As for assets other than your primary residence, the government does not want us sheltering our assets just before we sign ourselves in for long-term care, so you must distribute your assets at least 5 years in advance of that occurrence.

Gift your savings to your children, gradually, years before you fall ill, and ask them to hold it for you in the eventuality that you will need it. One strategy would be to make annual gifts to any of your children (the limit is currently $14,000 per year, per child). Ask them to set this money aside for your support and not spend it, in case you need it in the future. Of course, this strategy puts your money in the control of your children, and is based on trust.

There will be different tax implications depending upon how you structure your assets, so do consult with your accountant about what makes most sense for you.

Simplify Inheritance with Joint Ownership and Named Beneficiaries

Any of your property can be jointly owned by you and another person (such as the person you want to inherit the asset). Financial assets (such as bank accounts and insurance policies) can be jointly owned, or assets owned by you alone can have beneficiaries named by you. If an asset has joint owners, or if a beneficiary is named, such assets can be automatically passed to the joint owner or beneficiary without going through probate.

Life insurance policies, real estate, bank accounts, and vehicles all can have co-owners and beneficiaries. It is only when an asset has just one owner, who is now deceased, that an asset will have to go through probate court. Probate is the process that determines, under the watchful eye of a court of law, ownership for property that has no owner.

CHAPTER 4

PEOPLE:
Gather These Documents

Collect the following documents for each member of the family.

- Health Care Proxy (see Chapter 1)

- Durable Power of Attorney (Chapter 2)

- Will and Hand-written Memorandum (Chapter 3)

- Birth & Death Certificates
  - To obtain certified copies of a birth certificate, contact the County of Birth.
  - Death certificates will be issued by the facility handling the final remains. Get 15 copies of the death certificate.

- Marriage Certificate
  - To obtain certified copies of a marriage certificate, contact the County of Marriage.

- Military Discharge
  - To obtain a copy of a veteran's military discharge papers, contact:
    The Department of Defense
    National Personnel Record Center
    9700 Page Boulevard
    St. Louis, MO 63132

- Passport

- Social Security Card (or a photocopy)
- Legal Name Change Document
- Additional Forms & Documents (as needed)
  › Personal Letter
    Each person can be invited to add a letter to the survivors that should be opened "in the event of my death."

CHAPTER 5

PEOPLE:
Record This Information

Collect the following information for each member of the family.

Personal Information & History

- First name
  - Middle name
  - Last name
  - Maiden name
  - Other names used
  - Date of birth
  - Place of birth
  - Social Security number
  - Mother's maiden name
  - Current photo

- Spouse/Partner
  - Name
  - Contact information

- Residence & Contact
  - Primary residence address
  - Mailing address, if different
  - Home phone
  - Cellphone

- Electronic Passwords
  - Cellphone passcode

- › Email address(es) and password(s)
- › Computer password
- › Tablet password
- › Password vault password
- › Voicemail password
- › Security code for residence alarm system

- Passport Number

- Automobile(s)
  - › Driver's license number, state
  - › Vehicle make/model/color/year/VIN number
  - › Vehicle license plate, state
  - › Insurance provider, policy number

- Health & Doctor(s)
  - › Primary physician name
  - › Insurance provider, policy or ID number
  - › Blood type
  - › Allergies
  - › Medical conditions
  - › Rx medications

- Pet(s)
  - › Name(s)
  - › Photo
  - › Veterinarian, insurance company & policy number, ID chip number

- Service Providers
  - › Attorney name & contact information
  - › Accountant name & contact information
  - › Employer name & contact information
  - › Airline frequent flier: airline, membership number,

password
- End-of-Life
  › Preference for disposal of their body
  › Funeral preferences

Evaluating Options for What To Do with Your Body After Death

My mother had arranged in advance for her body to be given to the local medical school for autopsy training. She selected this option because it would have resulted in zero cost to her children after her death.

At 4 a.m., shortly after our mother died (in a hospital that was not in the town where our mother had resided and made plans), we telephoned the cellphone number our mother had provided, calling the medical school representative who was in charge of the body donation program. The director of the program did answer his phone at that early hour, and asked us a few questions about the condition of Mom's body at the time of death. He informed us that her body was not in proper condition for medical school purposes.

The hospital personnel then asked us, "What shall we do with her body?" Remember, it was 4 in the morning, and my sister and I had been with Mom all night. We were both from out-of-state and had no local knowledge. We had no answer; we knew only that funerals were reputed to be extremely expensive—which is why our mother had arranged to have her body donated to science for no cost. She had not formulated a Plan B.

We conferred with the hospital staff, and appreciated the suggestions given to us by several nurses. Within an hour, as the new day dawned, we had spoken to three possible facilities and made a choice for our mother that fit her criteria, budget, and location (there would be a charge for transport of the body from the hospital to the next facility).

The decision about what should be done with your dead body is one of your most personal decisions. A few months after my mother's death, as I made inquiries about cremation and burial options for myself, in a different state, I learned that procedures after a death vary state by state. Inquire locally about your options, and check with at least three providers. Some states offer "Green" burial options.

Inform yourself about your state law. Consider the costs, and how they will be covered. Then write down what your wishes are, and include this information in your READY BOOK.

CHAPTER 6

PEOPLE:
List Extended Family Contacts

Provide a list of family members who should be contacted.

Print out a paper list of family members and close friends who might be contacted in case of an emergency or death. Remember, your smartphone (where all your Contacts are stored) may not be functioning in an emergency. Also, not everyone in your contacts list needs to be informed of your death. In our mother's case, after she had decided to stop medical treatment, she gave us names of just a handful of friends who should be notified of her passing.

Make a list of the people who should be informed of your death. For each person, include:

- Name
- Phone
- Email

CHAPTER 7

PLACES:
Gather Documents & Keys

Collect the following documents and extra keys for each place you inhabit.

Whether you rent or own your residence, each of us may be responsible for multiple PLACES. In case of an emergency or death, others may need to deal with our PLACES.

Perhaps they need access to care for our pets while we are hospitalized, or access to belongings you need in your short-term rehab facility. Maybe you will be moved to a nursing home and will not be returning to your rented apartment, which must be vacated. After an owner has died, heirs may need to alter a deed or list a property for sale.

Legal Documents

Collect the following legal documents for your PLACES. If these documents are kept in a safe deposit box or some other secure location, specify where the documents can be found and how to access them:

- Real estate property deeds and titles
- Mortgage documents
- Insurance policies (homeowners, renters, auto or other vehicles)

Provide Access

In your READY BOX, provide PHYSICAL ACCESS (keys, combinations, and codes), and/or give directions to where to find the keys to your PLACES:

- Residence door key, with address and security code

- Business door key, with address and security code

- Storage door key, with address and security code

- Safe Deposit Box key, with bank name and address

- P.O. Box key, with post office box location

CHAPTER 8

PLACES:
Record This Information

Record the following information about your PLACES.

Residential Places

- Places you OWN:
  - Address
  - Owners on deed
  - Current estimated market value
  - Original purchase date and amount
  - Refinanced mortgage date and amount
  - Mortgage(s) on property
  - Mortgage lender
  - Lender phone number
  - Loan number
  - Original loan amount
  - Loan balance
  - Contract maturity date and predicted actual maturity date
  - Loan payment, escrow amount, P&I, interest rate

- Places you RENT:
  - Address of rented residence
  - Landlord contact
  - Lease document
  - Instructions for making a rent payment (amount, to whom, payment date)

Non-Residential Places

- Storage Unit
  - Address
  - Contact information
  - Contract number
  - Payment information (amount, payment date, payable to whom)
  - Location of the key to the storage unit

- Safe Deposit Box
  - Bank name
  - Address
  - Signers with access
  - Location of the key to the safe deposit box

- P.O. Box
  - Post Office location
  - Box number
  - Location of the key to your post office box

CHAPTER 9

PLACES:
Include Place History

Make a list of your previous residential addresses.

Besides being of personal interest to survivors, you will need this list to properly answer security questions posed by the three major Credit Monitoring Agencies, to verify your identity.

In order to determine that you are, indeed, who you claim to be, a typical security question from one of the major credit reporting companies may ask:

WHICH OF THE FOLLOWING IS A PREVIOUS ADDRESS FOR YOU?

_____ 16 Harrow Street
_____ 548-20 Kuuanupali
_____ 118 Westridge
_____ 22980 Shingle Circle
_____ None of the above

In checking your credit report for possible fraudulent activity, it's quite probable that your spouse or children or sister may not know (or may not remember) every address where you have resided over the last (in my case) 50 years. In addition, the question posed may offer a correct street name but an incorrect house number.

Provide a list of your previous addresses in the READY BOOK and make this question answerable!

Chapter 10

THINGS:
Take a Photo Inventory

Photograph every important item in your possession.

As we live our everyday lives, we accumulate things. Some are precious to us, and some lose their usefulness after a very short time. Those things that are not used every day are stored for that day in the future when we need them again.

We never expect to lose everything all at once, but news accounts of recent flooding and wildfires and mudslides remind us that it is possible for our real goods to simply disappear.

Make It Easy To File a Credible Claim of Property Loss: Photograph Everything

Photograph your yard and the exterior of buildings. Photograph your vehicles, inside and out. Open every drawer and cupboard, every closet and basement bin, even the refrigerator and freezer—and photograph the general contents.

Photograph each room from all sides. Photograph individual pieces of significant furniture, jewelry, clothing, equipment, tools, appliances, musical instruments, and artwork.

If you have family heirlooms that you intend to pass down to your heirs, take good photographs of those irreplaceable items.

Photograph the labels of your medical prescriptions.

If you should lose everything in an emergency, you will not remember exactly what you had.

Back Up Your Photos

Back up these photos in several places: on the Cloud, and on a photostick inside your READY BOOK. If you're lucky, you won't need them for years.

Chapter 11

THINGS:
Gather These Documents

*Collect proof-of-ownership documents for
all your valuable possessions.*

Our attorney tells us that vehicles are the possession most often left out of a Living Trust, and they often have a sole owner—so these one-owner vehicles must go through probate in order to be given a new owner after a death. If there is no joint owner on the vehicle, if there is no beneficiary listed in a Will or Memorandum, if the vehicle is not included in the Living Trust, your brother cannot just "take" the car. The probate court must declare your brother the owner.

On the other hand, if your vehicle is registered to joint owners (the not-yet-deceased YOU and the brother, for example), ownership is automatically transferred upon your death to the surviving joint owner without going through probate. Your brother already owns the car.

Collect proof-of-ownership documents for the following:

- Automobiles
  - Titles (automobiles and other vehicles)
  - VIN
  - License plate number, state
  - Registered owner(s)
  - Bill of sale or lease

- Jewelry
  - Proof of ownership and appraisals

- Art
  - Proof of ownership and appraisals

- Furniture
  - Proof of ownership and appraisals

- Musical Instruments, other equipment
  - Proof of ownership and appraisals

Chapter 12
THINGS:
Plan for Precious Belongings

Make a plan for the items you treasure.

As you photograph your things, pay attention to those that feel like family treasures. Consider what you might want most if you have just a few minutes to put a few items in your car and then leave for the evacuation route.

If possible, make it easy to grab your most precious belongings when the alarms go off.

Chapter 13

MONEY:
Make a Basic Financial Plan

Don't layer a financial crisis on top of another emergency. Prepare a basic financial plan for future emergencies.

I am the money person in our marriage. My husband has never once logged in to the bank website or worked inside our financial software program. If I should suddenly die or become incapacitated, my husband will probably not immediately wonder about the bank balance. It could be weeks before he thinks to check the bank. A financial train wreck would make any other emergency or difficult event even worse.

In this world of electronic banking, there's more to financial security than having a bag of cash under the mattress. I think there's a financial crisis waiting to happen—silently, invisibly—in the effortless, instant ebb and flow of our electronic cash.

Most of our financial transactions now happen online. Deposits and bill-paying are scheduled transactions that happen in our bank account even if we are not looking. I actively monitor our bank accounts online... but my husband has never done so. And that means it's not even in his consciousness to look.

Our income arrives in the bank unseen by us; we trust it to be there. Our mortgage and insurance premiums and credit card balances are paid automatically without any action on our part. So easy and efficient!

In our case, my spouse and I count on the income from two Social Security checks. What happens if I die and suddenly there is only one check, but the auto-paid bills keep on going? Worse, being electronic, this change would be invisible until such time as the bank found a way to let my husband know he was in arrears. (In the old days, a person at the bank would telephone us if a check was going to bounce. Today, a check may bounce and the bank will assess a fee, but, until I am looking at our account online or the mail brings an overdraft notice several days after the event, I will not know it has happened.)

As the person in the family who manages the finances, I have a responsibility to prepare for the day when I am not in charge. So what information about our money can I leave behind that will be most helpful to my husband, and allow him to move forward in his own way? How do I GET READY to hand over our money to my spouse's control?

For me, the plan includes creating some overview documents to explain our basic situation.

Chapter 14

MONEY:
Have Cash on Hand

In the weeks after an emergency or death, survivors should meet with an accountant to discuss how your financial resources can be used to maintain a level of security. The information you include in your READY BOOK will make their conversation with an accountant easier.

Right away, however, the family may need cash to get through the emergency. In each family, there may be only one person who has a clear overview of your financial resources and knows what the day-to-day cash flow is. If a large sum of money is needed to get through a crisis over several months, it will be helpful to the family to know what money is available, and where the potential sources are.

All the experts suggest that every family should have enough cash on hand to cover three months' expenses, at a minimum. Having such a financial cushion would indeed make a huge difference in our ability to Start Over, or Clean Up, or Endure the Shutdown, or just allow a surviving spouse to Move On.

Be determined—even if it is only a small amount every week, set aside cash, or a bank savings account with named beneficiaries—to build a cushion for emergencies. Set aside a portion every time you receive income.

Keep your emergency cash somewhere secure—and make sure your spouse and other relevant family members know how to access that safe spot.

CHAPTER 15
MONEY:
Gather These Documents

Collect the following documents to have easily accessible.

- Tax returns, most recent two years
- Bank statements, most recent months
- Mortgage statement or residential lease

CHAPTER 16

MONEY:
Document Your Assets

Create these documents to paint a useful picture of your financial situation.

Bank Accounts and Cryptocurrencies

Let survivors know where your assets are, and how to access them—or some assets may become invisible forever.

Here's an extreme example: In early 2019, it was reported that the founder of a Canadian crypto exchange died without sharing with anyone the password to his users' wallets. As a result, his customers may have lost access to their investments, valued at $190 million.

Whether you have one bank account or 20, make a list of the following for each account:

- Bank name(s), location

- Account number(s)

- Type of account

- Primary owner—Whose Social Security number is attached to each account?

- Signers, joint owner(s), beneficiaries
    › Who has access to your bank accounts? Ask your bank officer about whether you need to name beneficiaries for

bank accounts—Transfer-on-Death (TOD) or Payable-on-Death (POD) beneficiaries. Ask the officer to educate you about how this is different from having joint ownership of accounts. Ask which would be better for you.

- Where can checkbooks be found?

If you bank online, provide:

- Online banking URL
- Username
- Password
- Security questions/answers

Life Insurance/Accidental Death Insurance/ Disability Insurance

If a policy exists, heirs should contact the insurance policy provider directly after a death. Beneficiaries will need to provide a death certificate as well as proof of their own identity. Disability insurance will have specific criteria that must be met.

For each insurance policy, list:

- Policy provider
- Policy number
- Policy amount
- Beneficiaries
- Contact information

If you access your policies online, provide:

- Website URL
- Username
- Password
- Security questions/answers

Retirement/Investment or Pension Accounts

In case of your death, your surviving spouse may be reassured by receiving a lump sum distribution of funds from your retirement fund. Include:

- Financial institution
- Contact information
- Account number
- Balance
- Beneficiaries

If you access your investments online, also provide:

- Website URL
- Username
- Password
- Security questions/answers

Social Security

IMPORTANT TO REMEMBER: The moment a person who has been collecting Social Security benefits dies, the benefits STOP. In fact, if a Social Security payment is auto-deposited after a recipient's death, the money has to be returned to the Social Security Administration (SSA).

Now, while you are alive, call Social Security, gather the following information, and include your notes in the READY BOOK:

- Ask the agent to look at your account and explain what happens if you die.

- Ask what happens if your spouse dies.

- Ask (if pertinent) what happens if your former spouse dies.

- Ask what benefits a spouse who survives you should expect.

- Ask what happens if you and your spouse die at the same time.

- Double-check the amount of your benefit: You may be entitled to a larger Social Security check.
  > If you are married, and both of you are living, ask Social Security to see if your award amount is as high as it can be. Some people collect less than they are entitled to. When both husband and wife collect Social Security benefits, if one person's benefit amount is considerably more than the other (as when one person has much higher lifetime earnings than the other), the person receiving the lower amount may be entitled to have their amount raised.

After a death, call Social Security after you have received the death certificate:

- Report the death.

- Ask what to expect moving forward—your benefit amount may change.
  - For a married couple, in the case of the death of one person, the surviving spouse may be able to collect a higher payment amount than they received before. For a divorced former spouse, there may be an upwards adjustment. Ask Social Security about this.

- Confirm the destination bank account where the Social Security check is direct-deposited. Make sure the payment to the surviving spouse will be deposited into an account for which the surviving spouse is the primary account holder (that is, the account is listed under their Social Security number—your bank can tell you which account to use).

Business (Including Online Businesses)

Provide basic information about any business you conduct, especially as a sole proprietor, and especially if there is income to claim. List:

- Business name

- Address

- Phone

- Website username and password

- Shopping Cart admin login username, password, and security questions/answers

- Payment Processing Service login username, password, and security questions/answers (such as for PayPal, where money might be waiting to be retrieved)

- Domain provider for Website URLs

Note: Payment Processing Services Are Not Bank Accounts

PayPal is the service where transactions to our Website shopping carts take place. PayPal is a service, not a bank. PayPal doesn't allow for joint ownership accounts, and has no provision for naming beneficiaries. Like us, you may have a balance greater than zero dollars in your individual PayPal account, and income may be accruing. In order to name an heir for this income, list your PayPal account in the Memorandum to your Will (see Chapter 3) and name a beneficiary. Remember to provide a login and password to the account. Better yet, put a recurring reminder in your calendar to remind you to transfer any income into your bank regularly so the money doesn't accumulate in a dead-end account.

CHAPTER 17

MONEY: Document Your Liabilities

Credit Cards

When a new credit card account is opened, even if there are several cardholders, the account is linked to only one Social Security number; that is, each account has a primary owner.

Investigate the primary ownership of each of your credit card accounts. Make sure each adult has one credit card under their own Social Security number.

For each credit card, list:

- Credit Card company

- Card number, expiration date, CVV Code (on the back)

- Primary owner

- Date statement closes

- Date/from which bank account the bill is paid; is it auto-pay?

- Online username and password

- Security questions/answers

Real Estate Loans (First and Second Mortgages, Home Equity Line of Credit)

These loans are tied to real property. For each loan, list:

- Mortgage lender

- Loan number

- Payment amount and due date

- If auto-paid, from which bank account

- Online Website URL, username, and password

- Include a printed mortgage statement or spell out payment details, escrow, payment date, and contact information.

- IMPORTANT: If real estate taxes and home owners insurance are paid from escrow as part of your mortgage payment, remember you may have to confirm with all providers annually, to ensure continuity of payments.

Other Loans

Do you have personal loans, student loans, vehicle loans? For each loan, list:

- Purpose of loan

- Lender

- Loan number

- Payment amount and due date

- If auto-paid, from which bank account

- Online Website URL, username, and password

- Include a monthly statement or spell out payment details, payment date, and contact information.

Voided Check

Put into the READY BOOK a voided check from your main checking account, for which you are the primary owner (that is, the account is set up under your Social Security number).

A voided check may be required to set up any new direct deposits. The voided check is where your survivors can find the bank name, its routing number and your account number.

Explain How Your MONEY Flows: List Auto-payments and Direct Deposits

Create a document to show the predictable ins-and-outs of cash flow over a typical month, showing which bills are auto-paid/date/amount/from which account and which income is direct-deposited/date/amount/into which account.

Household Budget

Leave a typical monthly budget in the READY BOOK.

If you can and wish to do so, after you have created and documented a typical monthly budget, add a second column showing an imaginary budget forecast that illustrates how the changed monthly income for a surviving spouse might require changes in spending.

Financial Software

If you use financial software to track your cash flow for tax preparation, include it in the READY BOOK:

- Name of the software you use
- Main password to the computer the financial software is on

- Name of the file where all your financial history is
- Username and password to open the files
- And, if you're really thorough: Provide screen-capture videos showing how you use your financial software, in real time. Put this video on your THUMB DRIVE.

Ask Your Bank About Survivorship for Your Bank Accounts

Just a few hours after my mother died, I was sitting on her bed, logged in to her online bank account (on which I was a "Signer"), cancelling all the auto-payments. I telephoned Medicare and Social Security. It was only two weeks before her rent was due, so we notified her landlord of Mom's death in order to avoid paying any more rent or utilities. Our goal was to preserve the small balance in her bank account, hoping the balance would cover any expenditures yet to come. Soon after, to our surprise, her bank locked access to the account. Mom had set up her account with us as signers in order to protect the balance and not have the account frozen but, in retrospect, we should have been made co-owners or beneficiaries to have access. Since terms and policies may differ from one institution to another, it is worth checking, then double-checking the status on all your accounts.

Sit with a bank officer now and ask them to clearly explain what will happen to your accounts when you die, and what happens if your spouse dies first (or whatever your scenario is). Tell the bank officer you are creating instructions for your surviving family members and ask what you should include. In our case, I learned that while my husband and I are both joint owners of our checking account at the credit union, our joint account is set up under my Social Security number. If I die first, my husband will have access to the account as an owner, but he still will need to have an account under his own Social Security number into which the credit union can transfer the funds. Then auto-deposits and auto-paid bills will need to be redirected to the survivor's account.

Ask your bank officer about whether you need to name beneficiaries for bank accounts—Transfer-on-Death (TOD) or Payable-on-Death (POD) beneficiaries. Ask them to educate you about how this is different from having joint ownership of accounts. Ask which would be better for you.

Leave Helpful Suggestions

All of our bills are scheduled to be paid in full every month. Some bills, like the mortgage, are a set, predictable amount each month. Others, like our utilities, telephone, and credit card bills, have a different balance every month. Since we don't enjoy giant vats of cash like Scrooge McDuck, I have automatic reminders set in my calendar to check balances or transfer money around. I am pretty sure my husband will never do this. He's going to need a lump sum and a reminder to sit down with our accountant and one of our children to come up with a plan.

If you have hidden a cash reserve to be used in case of an emergency or death, leave this information behind, in the READY BOOK. If your cash reserves are not large enough to cover 6 months into the future, and if you can imagine what some of the challenges and solutions might be for your surviving spouse, put your thoughts in writing... in the READY BOOK.

CHAPTER 18

Help Family Access Your Devices & Data

Give your family access to all your devices.

About three weeks into our mother's final medical emergency, my sisters and I realized that Mom would not be returning to the apartment where she had been living independently. It was two weeks before her next month's rent would be automatically withdrawn from her bank account. We siblings had to decide if we should keep her apartment for one additional month, or if we could act quickly enough to vacate her residence. Could we immediately give notice and end all accumulating bills? We decided to end her financial commitments, and were able to accomplish this in one afternoon because we had online access to her bank accounts, credit cards, and utility accounts. We had her list of passwords and phone numbers in Mom's little green suitcase.

Computer Passwords (Including Tablets, Smartphones, Printers, Routers, and Websites)

In addition to sharing a printed, alphabetical list of all your passwords, you can set up an online password vault for free in LastPass.com, and even set up trusted family members with emergency access to your LastPass vault.

Even if you have given a family member emergency access to your password vault, include a print version in the READY BOOK. Devices may not always be accessible! My password document includes security questions/answers for each Website.

Be sure to include the MAIN passwords to unlock your devices:

- Desktop computer
- Laptop computer
- Tablet
- Smartphone
- Voicemail
- Modem
- Access point
- Printer
- LAN network
- Wifi

CHAPTER 19

In Case of Death, a Checklist: To Do IMMEDIATELY

This list of prioritized tasks will help you move more smoothly through the time immediately following a death in the family.

There will be immediate expenses for care of the body and a funeral. There may also be travel and accommodation expenses for family members, and the expense of feeding people. If there is money that has been set aside for this purpose, let your loved ones know:

There is $ _____ cash in the following location:

_____

Physical & Funeral

Is organ donation desired? The Health Care Proxy agent may have participated in this discussion with the deceased's physicians.

☐ Notify the deceased's doctor, if they have not already been involved.

☐ Follow body bequeathal instructions as determined by the deceased, or by the agent with the Durable Power of Attorney.

☐ Collect the deceased's personal belongings, if the death occurred away from home. Secure the deceased's property (pets, automobile, home, jewelry).

☐ Get 15 death certificates from the funeral home.

☐ Start talking with the family about a funeral.

☐ Prepare an obituary, especially if you will announce a funeral. Keep the listing short and to the point. Be cautious about posting death information on social media—use direct messaging instead of public posts. Do not share publicly any information that could be used by identity thieves and burglars.

Bank & Money

☐ Any of the deceased's assets that were placed into a Living Trust will pass directly to the heirs; a documented heir may visit the bank where the deceased's accounts were held and close the accounts and collect the balances without delay.

☐ If the deceased's accounts were owned jointly or have named beneficiaries, the surviving spouse/beneficiary should go to their bank(s) with a death certificate and meet with a bank officer (see the MONEY section). You may need to transfer funds from accounts owned jointly under the deceased's Social Security number into comparable accounts under your own (survivor's) Social Security number. Note that the transition of automatic electronic deposits and withdrawals from one bank account to another may take up to two months, so leave an ample balance in the original account to cover expenses during this period.

☐ The surviving spouse should ask the bank for the following numbers, and write them down; they will be needed to set up new direct deposits and auto-paid bills (see MONEY). The first changes will be for Social Security, if the deceased was receiving monthly benefits. Changing Social Security is an immediate priority, as benefits to the deceased stop immediately upon their death.

Bank routing number: _____

Redirect direct deposits that formerly went to this no-longer-pertinent account number: _____

INTO this new destination account number (owned by the survivor): _____

If you had a joint checking account with the deceased, that account will still be viable for a while; your changes to assign a new destination account for auto-withdrawals and auto-deposits may take up to two months to occur. Leave a cushion in the joint checking account so no transactions are refused. Once the new changes have all taken place, you can close the original joint checking account and move the remaining balance to the new account.

☐ Call life insurance provider or retirement account manager. (Check the MONEY section.) They will need a death certificate and proof of your identity.
On your call:

☐ REQUEST an immediate withdrawal of $_____

☐ ASK: What is fastest way to get these funds?

You may opt to leave a balance in the retirement account now and revisit its distribution at a later date.

Social Security

☐ Call Social Security at 1-800-772-1213

> Even if the deceased was not yet collecting Social Security benefits, this unique identifying number is the key to protecting one's identity. Notify Social Security of the death. Have at the ready when you call (all documents are in this READY BOOK): Deceased's birth and death certificates, survivor's birth certificate, marriage certificate, Social Security numbers (deceased and spouse).

On your call with the Social Security representative:

☐ ASK: What are your survivor benefits?

☐ ASK about the one-time death benefit ($255).

☐ ASK: What is the monthly amount you will receive moving forward? On what date?

☐ CONFIRM: Arrange for the NEW Social Security payment to be a direct deposit to a bank account opened under your (the survivor's) Social Security number.

☐ ASK: Do you owe a repayment? Any recent Social Security direct-deposit for the deceased may have to be returned to the SSA if it was deposited after the death.

☐ Spouse, arrange for your own Medicare Supplement insurance premium to be auto-paid from the account where your new Social Security payment will be deposited.

CHAPTER 20

In Case of Death, a Checklist: To Do TWO WEEKS Later

These tasks should be addressed fairly soon after the death of a loved one.

Begin to Rearrange Your Financial and Legal Matters

☐ If you have a mortgage that is paid automatically, redirect the mortgage auto-payment to the appropriate checking account.

☐ If applicable, notify the Veterans Administration to inquire about survivor benefits.

Contact Your Attorney

Meet with your attorney to go over what needs to be done. If another person is the executor of the deceased's estate, that person may accompany you. Take the READY BOOK binder with you.

Attorney name:_____

Attorney phone number: _____

☐ ASK: Must we go through probate?

☐ If yes, get "letters testamentary" (proof of executor).

☐ ASK: Help me understand what my fiduciary and other responsibilities are.

☐ ASK: Discuss the deceased's indebtedness: Which debts must be paid?

☐ ASK: Are there any debts of the deceased's that we do NOT have to pay?

☐ ASK: Does my own Will/Power of Attorney/Health Care Proxy need to be amended?

☐ ASK: Do my deeds and titles need to be amended to reflect a new joint owner?

Contact Your Accountant

Call or meet with your accountant to go over what needs to be done. If another person is the executor of the deceased's estate, that person may accompany you. If you are meeting in person, take the READY BOOK binder with you.

Accountant name: _____

Accountant phone number: _____

☐ ASK: What are the tax implications of this death?

Notify Others of the Death

☐ Notify close friends of the deceased and extended family (see the PEOPLE section).

☐ Use direct messaging to notify social media friends about the death rather than making a general public social media post. Then shut down the deceased's social media accounts, as you would any other account; passwords can be found in the deceased's password document. Be aware that identity thieves may utilize information you make public.

☐ Stop the deceased's health insurance (Medicare, Medicare Supplement, dental/vision insurance).

☐ Notify the Post Office.

☐ Call one of the three Credit Reporting Agencies (CRA): Experian, Equifax, or TransUnion. A deceased person's credit file will not be closed automatically; you must close their file. Request that the CRA update the credit record to indicate that the person is deceased. Any of the CRAs will then inform the other two agencies. The CRA will give you specific instructions on what to do. This notification should provide protection and prevent any other random person from using the deceased's ID to obtain credit.

Review Your Financial Situation

If you need help understanding your budget and cash flow, enlist the help of another family member.

☐ Review the documents in the MONEY section of the READY BOOK, showing all bank accounts, electronic deposits and withdrawals and a sample monthly budget.

☐ Review bills. Examine three months prior bank account statements for all your bank accounts (online or print) to identify bills that are paperless withdrawals. Close merchant accounts that are no longer necessary.

☐ Redirect auto-paid bills that still pertain, to your own account, if the destination bank account is different than before. (See the MONEY section)

☐ Project monthly income moving forward. Compare with projected monthly bills and make adjustments to your new budget.

☐ Checkbooks can be found in the following location: _____ .
Order a new checkbook for your new account if needed.

☐ Let your family know: I have/have not (circle one) made video directions to simplify things for you on how to use the financial software on my computer (see MONEY).

CHAPTER 21

In Case of Death, a Checklist: To Do 6 WEEKS – 6 MONTHS After

These tasks are less urgent and can be completed during the six months following the death of a loved one.

☐ Close or change joint credit card accounts to single accounts. Ask your attorney if all credit card account balances have to be paid in full. Note: If a credit card is linked to frequent flier miles, redirect the miles to yourself if you can.

☐ Cancel deceased's driver's license.

☐ Cancel deceased's social media accounts.

☐ Notify the Election Board.

☐ Notify additional family members and friends.

☐ Change title of vehicle. (Add a joint owner?)

☐ Change names on mortgage. (Add a joint owner?)

☐ Change names on bank accounts. (Add a joint owner?)

☐ Correct names on all utility accounts (telephone, internet, cable, electricity, gas, water).

☐ Cancel or change name on subscriptions.

☐ Make decisions about retirement account.

☐ Review monthly budget (see MONEY) and plan how to live on new projected monthly income.

☐ Sort through the deceased's personal belongings unless they have to go through probate. If you have any questions about this, call your attorney (see PEOPLE).

☐ IMPORTANT: Shred important documents instead of putting them in the trash.

CHAPTER 22

Where Should You Store Your READY BOOK?

Determine the physical container for your most important papers.

You began your READY BOOK by collecting your essential documents—your Health Care Proxy and your Durable Power of Attorney—into one, brightly colored and ready-to-go folder.

Once that was in place, you gradually added to the collection a range of documents that will help your loved ones move forward in a Medical, Property, or Financial Emergency, or in the case of a Death in the family.

How do you package up these precious files? Where do you keep them? What are you getting READY for?

Worst Case Scenario: Get Ready to Lose Everything

You must evacuate with no advance notice, and your home will be completely destroyed. You're grabbing your children, pets, wallet, medications, and cash—and racing to outrun the impending threat. You have just minutes, no time to think.

This scenario may seem far-fetched, but look to the experience of the residents of Paradise, California in the 2018 Camp Fire, or the residents of communities across the U.S. whose homes have been destroyed by floods or hurricanes or tornadoes or mudslides.

You're prepared. Your READY BOOK is already where you need it: in the Cloud. As you collected documents and information over the last year, you photographed everything with your phone and backed it up in the Cloud.

No matter what manufacturers claim, no "fireproof" or "waterproof" safe from the local big box building supply store will survive the most extreme storms. So, yes, collect the files. And yes, back them up in the Cloud. And think about what things are most important to you, and store those items with evacuation in mind.

You've planned ahead. You collected your essential information, photographed everything, and backed up your essential files in the Cloud. You also shared instructions with key family members about how to access the backup in case of emergency.

Get out of town!

Every Other Scenario: Get Ready to Operate in Confusing and Emotional Situations

Provide yourself and your family peace of mind by giving them easy access to all your critical documents and data to use in an emergency. Encourage them to do the same.

Let's say it's Friday night, and YOU (the family manager person) fall off a ladder putting up the holiday decorations, and you crack your head. Your Health Care Proxy agent will be able to work with your medical team and the insurance people, thanks to the legal permissions granted in this legal document.

It will be a while before you return to your regular life (if you ever do). In the meantime, while you are focused on recovering, other family members will assume the management of the household, using the information they find in your READY BOOK. Your loved ones can add these extra responsibilities to their regular lives because you have made it easier for them.

Photograph Everything in Your READY BOOK

In addition to taking photos of your Places and Things, photograph every document in the READY BOOK, then back up these photo files on an external photostick and in the Cloud. This backup redundancy is good protection.

Make sure your backups are in a secure location. And then share instructions about how to access the backups with your family. For future reference.

Select a Container for Your READY BOOK Collection

Now that you have collected everything that belongs in your READY BOOK, decide what kind of container will serve you best.

My Mom used a little green suitcase (actually, I think it's a piece of luggage known as a train case). There was plenty of room inside to hold her modest collection of documents, and it had a combination lock (set to her birthday) and a sturdy handle. It was certainly not fireproof or waterproof, but it did blend into the contents of her closet and did not call attention to itself. It was also easily portable.

For myself, I bought 1) a heavy-duty binder with clear plastic sleeves (an art portfolio), to store papers, 2) a set of hanging files for oversized papers (like loan documents, insurance policies, and tax returns), and a thumb drive to hold all the READY BOOK files I created on my laptop.

I decided to store my READY BOOK collection in a fireproof, waterproof container: I use a locking "safe" box that I bought at a big box building supply store. It is sufficient to hold my READY BOOK binder and files in hanging folders, but, weighing 60 pounds, it is too heavy to be considered "portable" in a fast evacuation.

And I doubt such a container would survive a monster fire like the Camp Fire—which is why photo backups in the Cloud are important.

If I must leave quickly, I plan to grab the READY BOOK binder from my box and GO. And if I never get to my READY BOOK, I'll reconstruct my life from the backups in the Cloud.

My READY BOOK container lives in a dry, accessible place in my basement, and (important!) my family knows where it is.

Why Use a READY BOOK? Why Not a Safe Deposit Box?

You may have some of your critical documents and items stashed in a bank safe deposit box. A safe deposit box may be the perfect place for expensive jewelry and cash. But some items (such as your Health Care Proxy and Durable Power of Attorney) should be easier to access.

What if an emergency takes place on a Friday night, just before midnight? What documents should be immediately available, even if the bank is closed? Those items should be moved to your READY BOOK, and they should be photographed.

Be sure your READY BOOK has a list of items stored elsewhere, such as items in a safe deposit box, and include access information.

Back Up Everything in the Cloud

Just in case the laptop I use (for everything!) is not among the items that are easily accessible in our emergency, I saved any computer files related to this READY BOOK onto a thumb drive that I taped to the inside upper lid of my READY BOOK container. I'm a little paranoid that a small thumb drive could fall into the box itself and no one would know to look for it, so I put it in a plastic bag and used duct tape to affix the bag to the inside of the top lid.

In the event all my physical files are destroyed, I have backed up all the READY BOOK files, as images, in the Cloud.

Write a Summary List of Contents for the Entire READY BOOK Container

Make the opening page of your READY BOOK binder a List of Contents of the entire container. This list will assist the distressed person who is looking for information.

Imagine this scenario: A medical emergency has happened. A family member, remembering what you said about the READY BOOK, opens the container and immediately sees a binder. The spine and the front of the binder has a label: **IN CASE OF EMERGENCY OR DEATH, LOOK HERE FIRST.** When the family member opens the binder, they immediately see the List of Contents, which describes everything in the binder, the hanging files, and the thumb drive.

Your distressed family member knows immediately that he will be able to help.

If you add documents to your READY BOOK or container, remember to update the List of Contents.

Place Your READY BOOK Container in its Permanent Location—and Show It to Your Loved Ones

Place your READY BOOK in a location where your loved ones will have access in case of emergency or death, and where, if necessary, a person can grab it quickly and GO. Leave it in its secure spot always. It may be years before it is needed, so don't move it around without telling your people!

And remind them: "Remember to LOOK IN THE READY BOOK."

Update Your READY BOOK When You File Your Taxes

Once you've submitted your tax return each spring, review your READY BOOK for changes, and update your contents.

This Is Your Most Confidential Information. Keep It Secure!

Realize that these are CONFIDENTIAL documents.

Do NOT take the entire binder to a hospital, or nursing home, or bank, or any public place where, if you set it down, someone else could pick it up.

DO take the entire binder to the attorney meeting and the accountant meeting for reference.

Remember: Every bit of identity-defining, critical, personal information is in here and should be protected. Keep the READY BOOK secure.

www.ingramcontent.com/pod-product-compliance
Lightning Source LLC
Chambersburg PA
CBHW071220070526
44584CB00019B/3096